OBJECTIVE MATERIAL SCIENCE

MULTIPLE CHOICE Q & A

RANJIT PRASAD

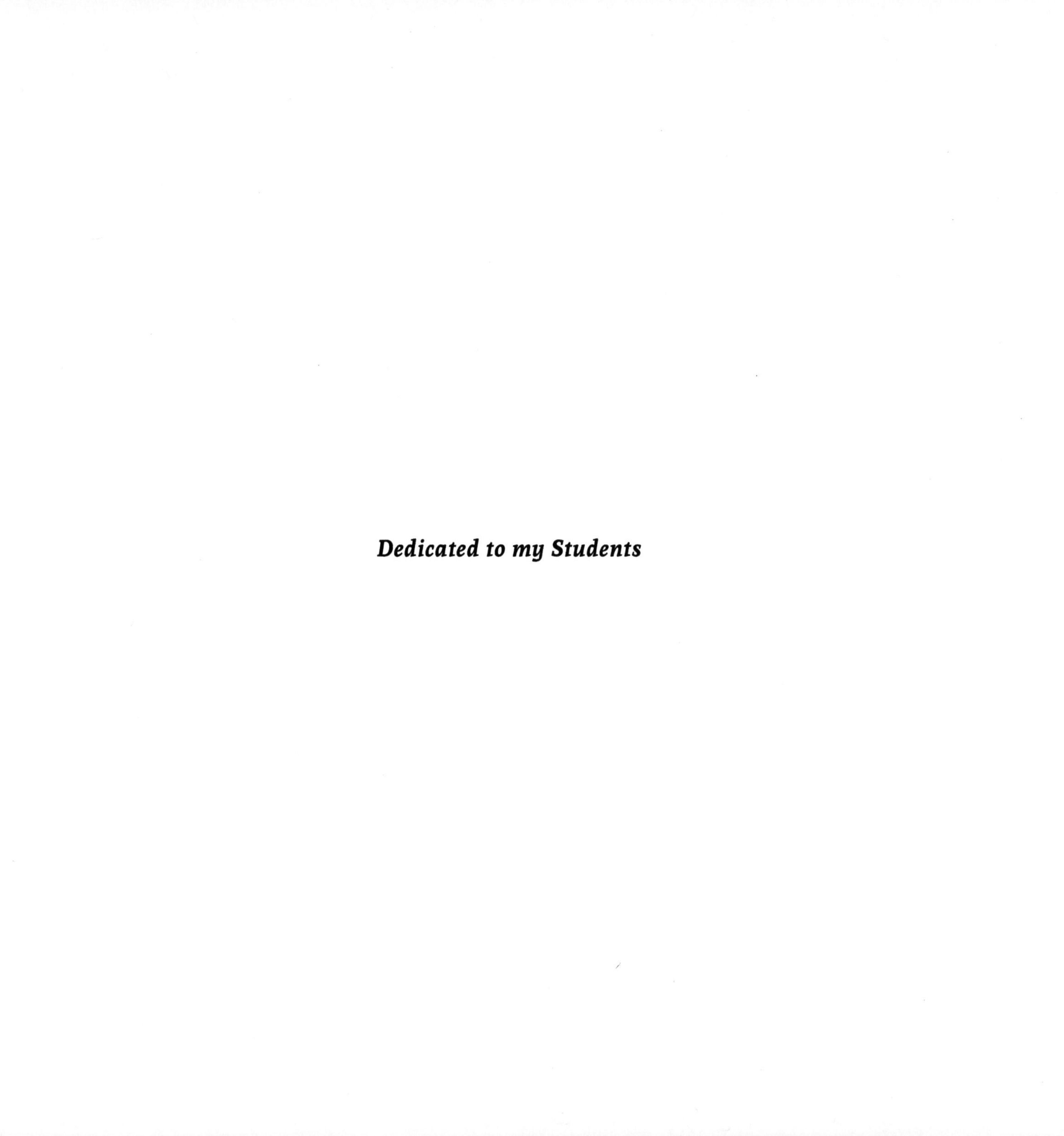

Dedicated to my Students

Contents

FOREWORD

Students will learn the fundamentals of material science from this book. This book is divided into two sections: short questions with answers and objective or multiple choice questions. This book addresses material science-related issues that are crucial to learning the fundamentals of the field.

The students would benefit from this book as they get ready for their Viva-voce and other competitive exams.

This book is an important addition to foundational studies on the fundamentals of material science and should be made available to a larger audience, both present and future, who are preparing for their exams.

Students studying chemistry, chemical, mining, geology, mechanical, and metallurgical engineering will find this book useful and self-sufficient as well.

(Dr.S Sen)

PREFACE

The understanding of material science will be aided by this text. Both objective and brief questions with their answers are included in the two sections of this book. This book addresses material science-related questions- answers that are pertinent to and helpful for comprehending the fundamentals of the discipline.

Additionally, this book will aid students in preparing for competitive exams such as Viva Voce.

This book is an important contribution to the fundamental research on the fundamentals of material science.

This book is helpful for the students who are studying chemistry, chemical, mining, geology, mechanical, and metallurgical engineering.

Acknowledgements

I take this opportunity to express my sincere thanks to my students of B.Tech Metallurgy at NIT Jamshedpur who contributed in collecting the questionnaire. I heartiest thanks to Suruchi who helped me in compiling the questions as well as uploading the same. My thanks are also to Archana Thakur and my brother Kishor Kumar Prasad, who reminded me time and again to write this book. Last but not least thanks to my wife Mrs Anita Prasad for compelling me to complete the present book.

Multiple choice Q & A

1. What is co-ordination Number?
a) It is the mass of an atom
b) It is the speed of an atom
c) It is the acceleration of the atom
d) It is number of nearest neighbors of the central atom in a structure

2. How many atoms constitute one unit cell of a face-centered cubic crystal?

a) 4 atoms

b) 5 atoms

c) 3 atoms

d) 1 atom

3. In which type of crystal system does MgCe belong?

a) Tetragonal crystal system

b) Cubic crystal system

c) hexagonal crystal system

d) None of the above

4. What is the co-ordination number in each type of ion in a "Rock Salt" crystal structure?

a) 5

b) 6

c) 7

d) 4

5. What is the co-ordination number of a unit cell whose packing efficiency is 68%?

a) 11

b) 13

c) 3

d) 8

6. What is the material from which Zinc Blende is obtained?

a) Zirconium

b) Sphalerite

c) Rutile

d) Wulfenite

7. What is void efficiency?

a) It refers to the nearest neighbours of the central atom in a structure

b) It is the percent of vacant space not occupied by particles in a unit cell

c) Both A and B option

d) Neither A nor B option

8. Aluminium crystallises in a FCC structure. Atomic radius of the metal is 125 ppm. What is the length of the side of the unit cell of the metal?

a)420 PM

b) 345.55 PM

c) 355.55 PM

d) 490.25 PM

9. Which crystal system has the highest volume of voids?

a) FCC

b) BCC

c) HCP

d) Simple Cubic

10. Which crystal system has the lowest volume of voids?

a) fcc

b) bcc

c) hcp

d) simple cubic

11. Lattice site in a pure crystal cannot be occupied by

a. Molecule
b. Ion
c. Electron
d. Atom

12. Total Number of tetrahedral void in fcc unit cell is?

a. 6

b. 8
c. 10
d. 12

13. What is Coordination number in square close packed structure in 2-D?

a. 2
b. 3.
c. 4
d. 6

14. Which type of surrounding lattice has when looked in particular direction?

a. Same
b. Different
c. Complex
d. None

15. Which is called simple geometrical arrangements of point?

a. Unit cell.
b. Crystal
c. Lattice
d. None

16. Which point is used for defining Unit cell?

a. Central
b. Lattice
c. Round
d. None

17. Which dimensions is used for describing space lattice?

a. 3-D
b. 2-D
c. 1-D
d. None

18. Nucleation _______ drastically as the temperature increases.

a. Decreases
b. Increases

19. The free energy needed for heterogeneous nucleation is equal to the product of homogeneous nucleation and a function of_____________:

a. the contact angle (θ)
b. critical radius

20. Heterogeneous nucleation differs from others due to ________

a. Faster rate of nucleation
b. Supercooling
c. Wetting
d. Growth

21. On which factor does the recrystallization temperature depend?

a. Purity
b. Density
c. Melting point
d. Grain size

22. Bakelite is an example of
a) elastomer

b) fibre

c) thermoplastic

d) thermosetting

23. The S in buna-S refers to
a) Sulphur
b) Styrene
c) Sodium
d) Salcylate

24. Gycogen, actually occuring polymer stored in animal is a
A) monosaccharide
B) disachharide
C) trisachharide
D) polysaccharide

25. Terylene is a condensation polymer of ethylene glycol and
A) benzoic acid
B) phthalic acid
C) dimethyl terephthalate
D) salicylic acid

26. Natural rubber in a polimar of
A) butadiene
B) ethyene
C) styrene
D) isoprene

27. Which of the following is a biodegradable polymer
A)cellulose
B) polyethene
C) pvc
D) Nylon-6

28. A polymer of butadiene and acrylonnitrile is called

A) Buna-2

B) Buna-n

C) Buna-S

D) buna-a

29. Zeigler-natta catalyst is used in making

A)LDPE

B) HDPE

C) polystyrene

D) PMMA

30. F2C=CF2 is a monomer of

A) teflon

B) glyptal

C) nylon-6

D) buna-s

31. Which of the following is used in tyre cords

A) Terylene

B) polyethylene

C) polypropylene

D) Nylon-6

32. Repeatable entity of a crystal structure is known as

(a) Crystal

(b) Lattice

(c) Unit cell

(d) Miller indices

33. Coordination number for closest packed crystal structure

(a) 16

(b) 12

(c) 8

(d) 4

34. Atomic packing factor is
(a) Distance between two adjacent atoms
(b) Projected area fraction of atoms on a plane
(c) Volume fraction of atoms in cell
(d) None

35. The atomic diameter of an BCC crystal (if a is lattice parameter) is
(a) a
(b) a/2
(c) a/(4/√3)
(d) a/(4/√2)

36. The packing fraction of simple cubic (SC) structure is about
a)52%
b)68%
c)25%
d)74%

37. Atomic packing factor for BCC is
a) 0.52 (SC)
b) 0.74 (FCC)
c) 0.68 (BCC)
d) None of these

38. Crystal type CsCl belongs to
a) BCC
b) SC
c) HCP
d) FCC

39. If the radius of an atom in a simple cubic crystal is r, the body diagonal of the unit cell is

a) r/√3
b) 2r/ √3
c) 4r/√3
d) 3r/4

40. Which of the following having highest packing factor?
a)BCC
b)simple cubic
c)FCC
d)FCC and simple cubic

41. Which of the following is an example of non crystalline solid?
a-Graphite
b-Sio2
c-chrome alum
d-silicon carbide

42. If hot silica is cooled slowly then it will become?
a-crystalline solid
b-amorphous solid
c- polycrystalline solid
d-cant say anything

43. Which is an example of amorphous solid?
a-Zns
b-Starch
c-metal
d-graphite

44. Which of the following is not an example of crystalline solid?
a-MgSo4
b-DNA
c-sugar
d-xenon

45. Amorphous solid posses-
a-sharp melting point
b-different physical properties
c-super cooled liquids
d-crystal symmetry

46. Crystalline solid are-
a-super cooled liquids
b- Anistropic
c-Isotropic
d-not sharp melting point

47. Which is an example of allotropic form?
a-Graphite and diamond
b-Rhombic and monoclinic
c-Quartz and feldspar
d-All of these

48. Which of the following axis system is being satisfied by cubic crystal system?
a) $a = b = c$, $\alpha=\beta=\gamma=90$
b) $a \neq b = c$, $\alpha=\beta=\gamma=90$
c) $a = b \neq c$, $\alpha=\beta=\gamma=90$
d)$a = b = c$, $\alpha\neq\beta=\gamma=90$

49. Which of the following axis system is being satisfied by tetragonal crystal system?
a) $a = b = c$, $\alpha=\beta=\gamma=90$
b) $a \neq b \neq c$, $\alpha=\beta=\gamma=90$
c) $a = b \neq c$, $\alpha=\beta=\gamma=90$
d) $a = b = c$, $\alpha\neq\beta=\gamma=90$

50. In tetragonal crystal system, which of the following is true?
a) All axial lengths and all axial angles are equal
b) All three axial lengths are equal
c) All three axial angles are equal

d) Two axial angles are equal but third is different

51. The atomic diameter of an BCC crystal is

a) a

b) a/2

c) a√3/2

d)a√2/4

52. Two substance that have same crystal structure-

a- isomorphous

b-Allotrope

c-polymorphous

d-Isotropes

53. Which is an example of true solid?

a-Plastic

b-Low density polythene

c-Glass

d- high density polythene

53. Which of the following is not an example of crystalline solid?

a-diamond

b-Radon

c-fused silica

d-Alloy

55. Which of the following compounds belongs to tetragonal crystal system?

a) ZnS, KCl

b) TiO2, CuFeS2

c) LiF , AgBr

d) Na2O, CuBr

56. What will happen with magnetic materials is kept in an external magnetic field?

a) They will move

b) They will develop magnetic lines of force
c) They will create a permanent magnetic moment
d) They will be unaffected

57. Magnetism originates due to rotational motion of charged particles.
a) True
b) False

58. What is the name of the continuous curve in the magnetic field, the tangent of which gives the direction of magnetic intensity?
a) Magnetic lines of force
b) Magnetic lines of induction
c) Magnetic force
d) Magnetic dipole moment

59. What is the name of the magnetic lines which forms a closed path?
a) Magnetic lines of force
b) Magnetic force between two poles
c) Magnetic field
d) Magnetic lines of induction

60. How is the residual magnetism from material removed?
a) Retentivity
b) Coercivity
c) Magneton
d) Switching off the magnetic field

61. In which of the following magnetic moment is zero?
a) Dia-magnetic material
b) Parra-magnetic material
c) Ferromagnetic material
d) Ferrimagnetic material

62. Which of the following is a weak magnet?
a) Ferromagnetic material

b) Antiferromagnetic
c) Paramagnetic
d) Diamagnetic

63. When does a diamagnetic material become normal material?
a) At critical temperature
b) Above critical temperature
c) Never
d) Below critical temperature

64. When does a paramagnetic material become diamagnetic material?
a) At critical temperature
b) Above critical temperature
c) Below critical temperature
d) Never

65. Magnetic susceptibility is negative for paramagnetic material.
a) True
b) False

66. Which of the following is true about the value of refractive index of quartz glass(SiO2)?
a) same in all directions
b) different in different directions
c) can't be measured
d) always zero

67. Which of the following is non-crytalline solid?
a) Mettalic(alloy)
b) Molecular (xenon)
c) Covalent(graphite)
d) non of these

68. If hot SiO2 is cooled quickly then it will become
a) crystalline
b) polycrystalline

c) amorphous
d) can't be say anything

69. Polymorphism is about:
a) whether a material union s crystalline or amorphous
b) whether a material can have multiple crystal structure
c) whether a material is solid or liquid
d) whether a material is single crystal polycrystalline

70. All crystalline material are characterized by
a) atoms packed in periodic arrays extending
b) transparency
c) an abrupt change in specific volume at the melting temperature
d) a and b

71. The point which shows the position of atoms in crystal are called as ....
a) crystal lattice
b) crystal parameter
c) bravis lattice
d) lattice point

72. The plane along which crystalline solid are broken down are called
a) cleavage plane
b) regular plane
c) irregular plane
d) simple plane

73. Anistropy is a material means
a) the same thing as isotropy
b) the crystal structure varies with temperatures and/or pressure
c) properties varies with directions
d) the material consist of many individual crystal oriented in different direction

74. Isomorphism is possible because of compatible
a) ratio

b) size
c) shape
d) color

75. The habit of the crystal is its
a) color
b) size
c) shape
d) density

76. "In which of the following boundaries,rotation axis is parallel to the boundary plane ?

i. Twist boundary ii.Twin boundary

iii.Tilt boundary iv.none of these."

77. Stacking fault energies are in the range of :
(a) 0.01-0.1 J/m2
(b) 0.01-0.1 J/cm2
(c) 0.1-10 J/m2
(d) 0.1-10 J/m2

78. "In which of the following boundaries,rotation axis is perpendicular to the boundary plane ?

i. Twist boundary ii.Twin boundary

iii.Tilt boundary iv.none of these."

79. For solidification, cooling the liquid below its melting point is

a)Sufficient, but not necessary condition

b)Necessary and sufficient condition

c)Neither necessary and nor sufficient condition

d)Necessary, but not sufficient condition

80. Heterogeneous nucleation is much easier to occur because

a)the surface energy term is much smaller during heterogeneous nucleation volume
b)energy term is much higher during heterogeneous nucleation

c) the surface energy term is much higher during heterogeneous nucleation

d) volume energy term is much lower during heterogeneous nucleation

81. What is the unit of thermal gradient?

a) cal/cm^2.°C

b) cal.°C/cm

c) cal/cm.°C

d) cal.cm.°C

82. Which of the following is true regarding homogeneous nucleation?

a) With increasing undercooling, nucleation rate decreases
b) With increasing undercooling (lowering of temperature), critical size of the nucleus decreases

c) With increasing undercooling, homogeneous nucleation becomes less and less probable

d) With increasing undercooling, ΔG increases

83. In nucleation, particles having radius less than rc are known as

a) Nuclei

b) Embryo

c) Element

d) Atom

84. During solidification of casting and ingots, total heat that needs to be taken out of the liquid for solidification, includes

a)Only the heat of fusion

b)Heat of fusion + heat given out by solidifying liquid

c)Heat of fusion + heat given out by solidifying liquid + extra heat in the liquid (called superheat)

d)Heat of fusion + extra heat in the liquid (called superheat)

85. What is the heat balance equation for liquid-solid interface?

a) Ks-Kl = Ps.HRT

b) Ks.Gs-Kl.Gl = Ps.RT

c) Ks.Gs-Kl.Gl = Ps.HR

d) Ks.Gs-Kl.Gl= Ps.2RT

86. Heterogeneous nucleation rate can be expressed by

a) Nhet. =n1.exp($\Delta G°$/ KT)

b) Nhet = f1.n1.exp(-$\Delta G°$/R.T)

c) Nhet = f1.n1.exp(ΔG°/T)

d) Nhet = f1.n1. exp(-ΔG°/K.T)

87. How is the critical radius of particles calculated?

a)Y/ΔF1

b)2Y/ΔF1

C)Y/vE

d)2Y/vE

88. For semi-infinite insulating mold condition, the plot between S and it is

a) Parabolic

b) Elliptical

c) Linear

d) Asymptotic

89. Nylon threads are made of

a. polyester polymer
b. polyamide polymer
c. polyethylene polymer
d. polyvinyl polymer

90. Which of the following is a branched polymer?

a. low density polymer

b. polyester
c. high density polymer
d. nylon

91. In addition polymer, monomer used is

a. unsaturated compounds
b. saturated compounds
c. bifunctional saturated compounds
d. trifunctional saturated compounds

92. Which of the following does not undergo additional polymerisation?

a. vinyl chloride
b. butadiene
c. styrene
d. all of the above undergoes addition polymerisations

93. Polymer formation from monomer starts by

a. the condensation reaction between monomers
b. the coordinate reaction between monomers
c. conversion of monomer to monomer ions by protons
d. hydrolysis of monomers

94. Which of the following statements is not correct for fibres?

a. Fibres possess high tensile strength and high modulus
b. Fibres impart crystalline nature
c. Characteristic features of fibres are due to strong intermolecular forces like hydrogen bonding
d. All are correct

95. Which of the following monomers form biodegradable polymers?

a. 3-hydroxybutanoic acid + 3-hydroxypentanoic acid
b. Glycine + amino caproic acid
c. ethylene glycol + phthalic acid
d. both a and b

96. On the basis of mode of formation polymers can be classified:

a. as addition polymers only
b. as condensation polymers only
c. as copolymers
d. as addition and condensation polymers

97. The process of heat softening, moulding and cooling to rigidness can be repeated for which plastics?

a. thermoplastics
b. thermosetting plastics
c. both (a) and (b)
d. neither (a) nor (b)

98. The polymer used in making hair synthetic hair wigs is made up of

a. $CH_2=CHCl$
b. $CH_2=CHCOOCH_3$
c. $C_6H_5CH=CH_2$
d. $CH_2=CH-CH=CH_2$

99. Which of the following do not belong to the type of silicon nitride ceramics?
1. Reaction bonded silicon nitride
2. Hot pressed silicon nitride
3. Stiff silicon nitride
4. Pressure-less Sintered silicon nitride

100. Which of the following is a characteristic of alumina Al2O3?
1. good Hardness
2. better Tensile strength
3. better Toughness
4. Poor Wear resistance

101. Which class of engineering ceramics generally includes lubricant materials?
1. Sulphides
2. Carbines
3. Metalloids
4. Inter Metallics

102. Which of the following Carbide are used for cutting tools?
1. Silicon carbide
2. Tungsten carbide
3. Vanadium carbide
4. Chromium carbide

103. Which step is irrelevant in making ceramics?
1. Powder pressing
2. Sintering
3. Alloying
4. Vitrification

104. Ceramic Materials are
1. soft
2. superconductor
3. weak
4. insulator

105. silicon carbide is?
1. Tensile strengthen
2. Oxidation resistive

3. Thermal Conductive
4. none of above

106. Glass can be considered as
1. Clay ceramics
2. Ceramic Material
3. Bound together
4. Pottery and Bricks

107. Which ceramic material does have this formula Si3Al3O3N5 ?
1. Silicon Carbide
2. Silicon nitride
3. SiAlON
4. Silicon aluminum nitrate

108. How is the creep strength of ceramics when compared to other materials?
1. Zero
2. Low
3. High
4. Excellent

109. The materials whose electrical conductivity is usually less than 1 × 10^6 mho/m are

a) Semiconductors
b) Conductors
c) Insulators
d) Alloys

110. Fermi Level is the energy where the probability of a state occupied in conduction and valance band is
a) 0.1
b) 0.5
c) 1.0
d) 0.33

111. The average energy of an electron in the conduction band of a metal at 0° K as a function of Fermi Level (EF) will be

a) 1/5 EF

b) 2/5 EF

c) 3/5 EF

d) 4/5 EF

112. The thickness of depletion region in semiconductor diode is of the order of

a) 1 × 10^-4 micron

b) 1 × 10^-6 micron

c) 1 micron

d) 1 × 10^-6 cm

113. The energy gap is maximum in

a)Conductors

b)Semiconductors

c)Superconductors

d)Insulators

114. With the increase in temperature the resistance of semiconductors

a)Decreases

b)Increases

c)Remains constant

d)Initially increases and then decreases

115. Fermi energy level for intrinsic semiconductors lies

(a) At middle of the band gap

(b) Close to conduction band

(c) Close to valence band

(d) None

116. Mobility of holes is ___________ mobility of electrons in intrinsic semiconductors.

(a) Equal

(b) Greater than

(c) Less than
(d) Can not define

117. Fermi level for extrinsic semiconductor depends on
(a) Donor element
(b) Impurity concentration
(c) Temperature
(d) All

118. Energy band gap size for semiconductors is in the range ________ eV.
(a)1-2
(b) 2-3
(c) 3-4
(d) > 4

119. Which branch deals the study of crystals only?
a.Mineralogy
b.Crystallography
c.Geomorphology
d.None of these

120. Which law is useful for measuring of wave length and for determining the lattice spacing of crystals?
a.Malus law
b.Brewster's law
c.Bragg Law
d.All of the above

121. Which is/are correct form of Bragg's equation?
a.$2d\sin\theta=(n+1)\lambda$
b.$2d\cos\theta=n\lambda$
c.$d\sin\theta=n\lambda/2$
d.$d\sin\theta=n\lambda$

122. At what angle for the first order diffraction spacing between has planes, respectively are λ and $\lambda/2$
a.0°,90°

b.90°,0°
c.30°,90°
d.90°,30°

123. Amorphous solid are
a.Isotropic and supercooled liquids
b.Isoenthulpic and superheated liquids
c.Anisotropic and supercooled liquids
d.Isotropic and superheated liquids

124. Crystals which are good conductors of electricity and heat are
a.Ionic crystals
b.Covalent crystal
c.Metallic crystal
d.Molecular crystal

125. The Bond length and bond angles in molecules in the solid state are called by
a.X-ray diffraction technique
b.Neutron bombardment
c.Proton bombardment
d.None of these

126. Bragg's equation is based on which technique?
a.X-ray refraction method
b.Alpha ray refraction method
c.X-ray reflection method
d.X-ray diffraction method

127. Isomorphic form of sodium sluride is
a.Chlorine
b.Magnesium oxide
c.Sodium
d.Sulphur

128. Which is not an example of amorphous?

a.Polystrene

b.Acrylic

c.Polypropylene

d.Polycarbonate

129. Mark the correct statement about the "Law of constancy of Interfacial-angle":

(a) The interfacial-angles of crystals of a particular mineral remain always constant.

(b) The atomic structure of the crystals of a particular mineral is fixed.

(c) The position of faces of the crystals of a particular mineral is equal.

(d) All are correct.

130: what is the normal interfacial angle in dodecahedron form of cubic system

(a)60°

(b) 45°

(c) 9 O°

(d) 120°

131:The crystals are bonded by plane faces (f)(f) straight edges (e)(e) and interfacial angle (c)(c). The relationship between these is

(a)f+c=e+2

(b)f+e=c+2

(c)c+e=f +2

(d)none of these

132:Who discovered the law constancy of interfacial angle?

(a)John Hasbrouck

(b)Hans Bethe

(c) Nicolas Steno

(d)none of these

133: Name device to measured interfacial angle

(a)Protractor

(b)laser measure

(c)goniometer
(d)none of these

134:In which of the following systems, interfacial angles α=γ=90o but β≠90o?
(a)Monoclinic
(b)Rhombohedral
(c)Triclinic
(d)Hexagonal

135:Interfacial angles do not depend upon.
(a)shape of crystal
(b)atoms in crystal
(c)colour
(d)outer

136:If all three interfacial angles defining the unit cell are equal in magnitude the crystal cannot be:
(a)rhombohedral
(b)cubic
(c)hexagonal
(d)tetragonal

137:Select the correct match about crystal system
Crystal system interfacial angle no. of bravais unit cell
(a)cubic system $\alpha=\beta=\gamma=90^{\circ}$ 4
(b)hexagonal $\alpha=\beta\neq\gamma$ 1
(c)orthorhombic $\alpha=\beta=\gamma=90^{\circ}$ 3
(d)Monoclinic $\alpha=\beta\neq\gamma$ 1

138:The interfacial angle of a hexagonal crystal system are given by
(a) $\alpha=\beta=\gamma=90^{\circ}$
(b) $\alpha=\beta=90, \gamma=120^{\circ}$
(c) $\alpha=\beta=\gamma\neq90^{\circ}$
(d) $\alpha\neq\beta\neq\gamma\neq90^{\circ}$

139. what are the classification of polymer on the basis of ther general structure

a)linear

b) branched

c) cross-linked

d) Network

e) all of the above

140. What is no of types of composites

a)3

b)4

c)5

d)2

141. What type of bond exist betn the molecules of thermo-plastics polymer

a) ionic bond

b) covalent bond

c) both 'a' and 'b'

d) non of the above

142. Example of thermo plastic ploymer is

a) nylon, polyethylene, rubber

b) epoxy, phenolics

c) both 'a' and 'b'

d) none of the above

143. What are the characteristics of Metals.

a)shape can be changed permanently

b) Good thermal conductivity

c) Good electrical conductivity

d) All of the above

144. Properties of polymer
a) high strength, ductile, thermal and electrical conductivity
b) low density, low melting point, ductile
c) high melting point, Good insulator, Corrosion resistant
d) All of the above

145. Materials can be
a) pure
b) impure
c) living or non-living matter
d)all of the above

146. while selecting material we should keep care about
a) design economic
b) asthetic demands
c) strength and durability
d) all of the above

147. According to nature of Engineering material we can classify it in _________ broad group.
a)two
b)three
c) four
d) five

148.What are the characteristics of Metals.
a)shape can be changed permanently
b) Good thermal conductivity
c) Good electrical conductivity
d) All of the above

149. Which are the to major components of material science and engineering
a)processing of materials
b) structure of materials
c) properties of materials

d) performance of materials
e) all of the above

150. Which type of bond does exist between the molecules of ceramic material
a) ionic bond
b) Covalent bond
c) both 'a' and 'b'
d) none of the above

151. Burger's vector changer with
A kind of dislocation
B length of dislocation
C both
D none

152. Which one is not a point defect
A stoichiometric defect
B screw dislocation
C non-stoichiometric defect
D impurity defect

153. Frenkel defect is caused due to displacement of

A cation

B anion

154. Which one is not a stoichiometric defect

A vacancy

B interstitial

C substitutional

D metal excess

155. If a non-metal is added to the interstitial sites of a metal then the metal becomes

A) Softer

B) Less tensile

C) Less malleable

D) More ductile

156. Point defects are present in

A) Ionic solids

B) Molecular solids

C) Amorphous solids

D) Liquids

157. Ionic solids, with Schottky defects, contain in their structure?

A) Equal number of cation and anion vacancies

B) Anion vacancies and interstitial anions

C) Cation vacancies only

D) Cation vacancies and interstitial cations

158. The flame colours of metal ions are due to?

A) Frenkel defect

B) Schottky defect

C) Metal deficiency defect

D) Metal excess defect

159. Which of the following phenomenon creates point defect in ceramics?

a) Thermal excitation

b) Precipitation

c) Densification

d) Electrical conductivity

160. Which of the following oxides are highly defective?

a) Al_2O_3

b) MgO

c) CaO

d) FeO

161. Sommerfield developed?

(a) Classical free electron theory.

(b)Quantum free electron theory.

(c)Zone theory.

(d) None of the above

162. Average drift velocity per unit Electron field strength is known as?

(a) Relaxation time.

(b) Mobility.

(c) conductivity.

(d)RMS velocity

163. According to classical theory , electron obey?

(a) Bose Einstein statistics

(b) Maxwell Boltzmann statistics

(c) Fermi Dirac statistics

(d) Planks law

164. Electron collision according to classical theory are?

(a) elastic

(b) inelastic

(c)none

(d)semi elastic

165. Specific heat of metals according to classical theory are

(a) 3R

(b)4R

(c) 3.5R

(d)4.5R

166. According to classical theory electrons move in

(a) Uniform potential field in the lattice

(b)Non uniform potential field in the lattice

(c) periodic potential field in the lattice

(d) sinusoidal potential field

167. Elements of crystal consists of ....

a) Angle and edge only

b) Angle,edge ,faces

c) Faces and edge only

d) None of these

168. One of the relatively flat surface by which a crystal is bounded are known as

a) faces

b) surface

c) plane

d) all of these

169. No. of faces in trigonal prism is

a) 3

b) 4

c) 5

d) 6

170. Angle between normal of two faces is known as

a) solid angle

b) interfacial angle

171. How many types of flat surfaces present in a crystal.

a) three

b) two

c) four

d) five

172. Intersection of two faces ina crystal is called ______.

a)edges

b)vertices

c)corner

d) none of these

173. The symmetry of crystal faces with respect to a line , plane and or point can be use to classify crystal into

a) crystal habit

b)closed or open forms

c) crystal interfacial angle

d) crystal system

e) none of the above

174. In a regular tetrahedron the angle between any two faces is

a) arcsin (1/3)

b) arccos(1/3)

c) arctan(1/√3)

d) arccos(1/√3)

175. The lines which are perpendicular to the crystal faces which makes the interfacial angle is called

a) poles

b) scalloped

c) dashed line

d) implied line

176. Unit of solid angle between two faces of crystal is measured in ________________.

a) radian

b) steradian

c) degree

d) gradient

177. Which one of the following statements about the (2(bar)41(bar)) and (24(bar)1) planes is false?

a They are perpendicular.

b They are part of the same set of planes.

c They are part of the same family of planes.

d They are parallel.

178. Does the [12(bar)2] direction lie in the (301(bar)) plane?

a Yes

b No

179. When writing the index for a set of symmetrically related planes, which type of brackets should be used?

a (Round)

b {Curly}

c <Triangular>

d [Square]

180. Which of the <110> type directions lie in the (112) plane?

a [110] and [11(bar)0]

b [101(bar)] and [101]

c [011] and [1(bar)01]

d [1(bar)10] and [11(bar)0]

181. What is the common direction between the (13(bar)2(bar)) and (1(bar)33) planes?

a [3(bar)10]

b [3(bar)1(bar)0]

c [4(bar)10]

d [4(bar)1(bar)0]

182. Which set of planes in a cubic-close-packed structure (such as copper) is close packed?

a {110}

b {100}

c {111}

d {222}

183. The atomic diameter of an BCC crystal (if a is lattice parameter) is

(a) a

(b) a/2

(c) a/(4/√3)

(d) a/(4/√2)

184. Atomic packing factor is

(a) Distance between two adjacent atoms

(b) Projected area fraction of atoms on a plane

(c) Volume fraction of atoms in cell

(d) None

185. A plane is parallel to an axis. What is its Miller Index?

a Infinity

b 0

c 1

186. The x-, y-, and z intercepts of a plane are 2,1, and 3. Its Miller Indices are

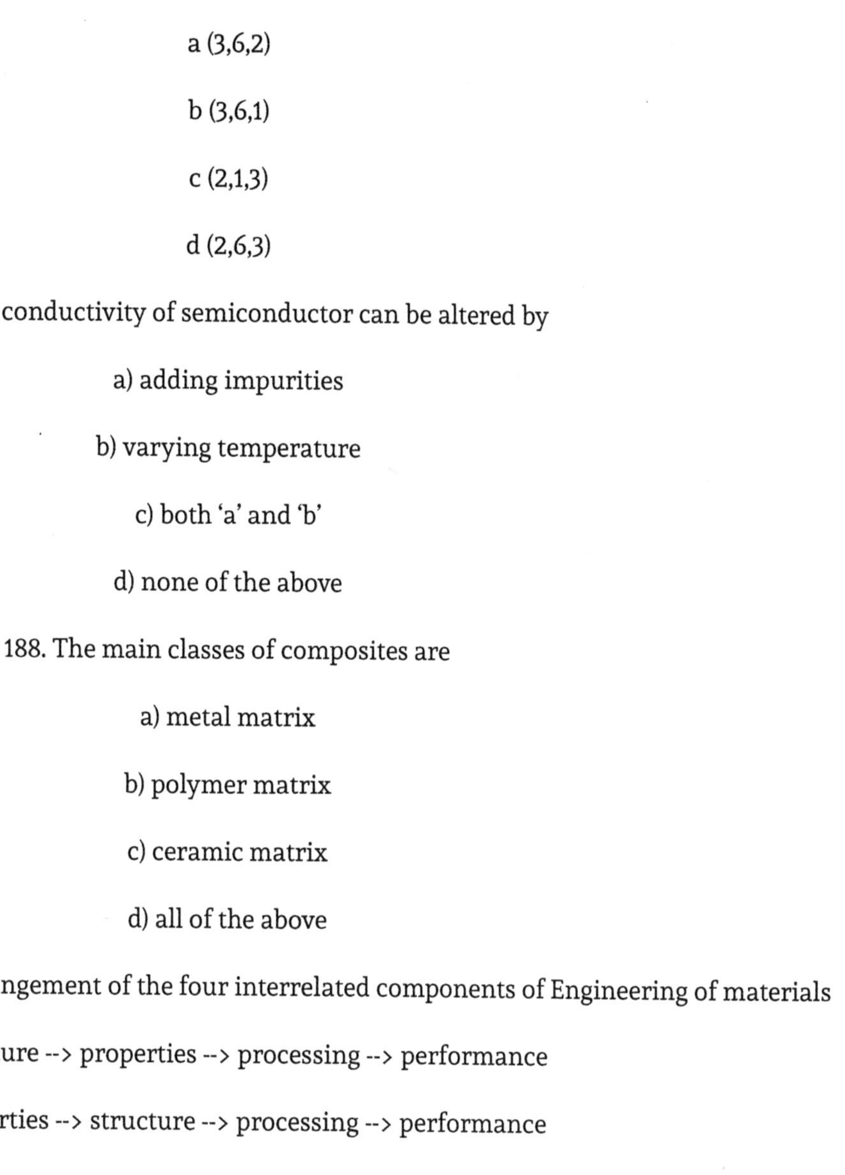

a (3,6,2)

b (3,6,1)

c (2,1,3)

d (2,6,3)

187. The conductivity of semiconductor can be altered by

a) adding impurities

b) varying temperature

c) both ‘a’ and ‘b’

d) none of the above

188. The main classes of composites are

a) metal matrix

b) polymer matrix

c) ceramic matrix

d) all of the above

189. Which one is the correct arrangement of the four interrelated components of Engineering of materials

a) Structure --> properties --> processing --> performance

b) properties --> structure --> processing --> performance

c) performance --> properties --> structure --> processing

d) processing --> structure --> properties --> performance

190. Which of the following material generally has lowest Tensile Strength ?

a) Metals

b) Ceramics

c) Polymers

d) Composites

191.Porcelain is an example of

1)whitewater ceramic

2)stone ceramic

3)abrasive ceramic

4) cement ceramic

192. major classes of engineering materials are-

1)metal, ceramic and semiconductor

2)polymer , metals and composites

3)metals, ceramic, polymers and semiconductor

4) metals, ceramic, polymers, semiconductor and composite

193.Which of the following is not a property of ceramics?

1)high strength

2) hing melting point

3) bad insulation

4) all of the above

194.Composite are classified on the basis of -

1) size and shape of reinforcement

2) type of matrix

3) both of the above

4) none

195.Major load carrier in dispersion- strengthen composites is -

1) matrix

2) fiber

3) both of the above

4)none of the above

196.temperature at which ceramics are mostly used in engineering ceramics(on average)?

1)260°c

2)815°c

3)1200°c

4)above 2500°c

197.Which one of the following is a step for making ceramic?

1) Splintering

2)Powder pressing

3)vitrification

4)all of the above

198.Corundum is type of -

1)Glass Ceramics

2)stone ceramics

3) refractories

4) abrasive ceramics

199.The composite constituents of both matrix and reinforcement are softer .

1) True

2) false

3) may be true in some case

4)above result cannot be possible

200.What type of combination combination of two or more materials having property different from each of components?

1)compound

2) composite

3) mixture

4)matrix

ANSWER KEY

1	2	3	4	5	6	7	8	9	10
d	a	a	b	d	b	b	c	d	a
11	12	13	14	15	16	17	18	19	20
c	b	c	a	c	b	a	a	a	c
21	22	23	24	25	26	27	28	29	30
a	d	b	d	c	d	a	b	b	a
31	32	33	34	35	36	37	38	39	40
d	c	b	c	c	a	c	b	a	d
41	42	43	44	45	46	47	48	49	50
b	a	b	b	c	d	b	a	c	c
51	52	53	54	55	56	57	58	59	60
c	a	a	c	b	c	a	a	d	b
61	62	63	64	65	66	67	68	69	70
a	d	d	c	b	a	d	c	b	d
71	72	73	74	75	76	77	78	79	80
d	a	b,c	a	c	3	a	1	d	a
81	82	83	84	85	86	87	88	89	90
c	b	b	d	c	d	b	c	b	a
91	92	93	94	95	96	97	98	99	100
a	d	a	d	d	d	a	a	3	1
101	102	103	104	105	106	107	108	109	110
1	2	3	4	4	2	3	4	c	b
111	112	113	114	115	116	117	118	119	120
c	c	d	a	c	d	d	b	b	c
121	122	123	124	125	126	127	128	129	130
c	c	a	c	a	d	b	c	d	a
131	132	133	134	135	136	137	138	139	140
a	c	c	a,b	a	a	b	b	e	b
141	142	143	144	145	146	147	148	149	150
b	a	d	b	d	d	b	d	e	a
151	152	153	154	155	156	157	158	159	160
d	b	a	d	b	a	a	d	a	d
161	162	163	164	165	166	167	168	169	170
b	b	b	a	d	a	b	a	c	b
171	172	173	174	175	176	177	178	179	180
b	a	d	b	a	b	a	b	b	d
181	182	183	184	185	186	187	188	189	190
b	c	c	c	b	a	c	d	d	c
191	192	193	194	195	196	197	198	199	200
1	4	4	2	1	4	4	4	2	2

Q & A

1. If I will Exchange The Crystals Of Enantiomorphous Crystals then Will it work Properly again as previous?

- No

2. Give An Example Of Enantiomorphous form Of Crystal.

- Quartz

3. Define Enantiomorphous form of Crystal.

- possessing neither a plane nor a center of symmetry, may occur in two positions that are mirror images of one another.

4. If we use Enantiomorphous form of crystal for Circular Polarization of Light will it works?

- Yes

5. Enantiomorphous is Simple Form Or Compound?

- Can be Both

6. Enantiomorphous quartz Are Closed Form Or Open?

- Closed

7. Which transformation starts after the nucleation of ferrite phase?

- Buinite transformation

8. The process of decomposing martensitic structure by heating martensitic steel below its critical temperature is called as-

- Tempering

9. Which process permit the transformation of austenite to martensite ?

- Martempering and Marquenching

10. Which method measures hardenability of a metal?

- Gross Man's method

11. In which method, surface of a steel component becomes hard due to phase transformation austenite to martensite ?

- Flame hardening

12. TTT diagram indicates time and temperature transformation of –

- Austenite

13. The purpose of normalising steel is to-

- Remove induced stresses

14. To reduce internal stresses of a hardened tool , the method of heat treatment generally applied is

- Tempering

15. In a case hardening process, ammonia gas is produced on steel, the process is known as

- Nitriding

16. Cyaniding and Nitriding are two methods of –

- Case hardening

17. Edge length of fcc in terms of radius of sphere is

- $2\sqrt{2}\,r$

18. Edge length of bcc in terms of radius of sphere is

- $4r/\sqrt{3}$

19. Edge length of simple cubic unit cell in terms of radius of sphere is

- 2r

20. Non-equilibrium phases are shown for their time and transformation by using which diagram?

- TTT and CCT diagram.

21. What does CCT diagram stand for?

- Continuous-cooling-transformation

22. What is used to predict quenching reactions in steels?

- Isothermal transformation diagram.

23. Austenising of samples for TTT diagram is done in which temperature?

- Above eutectoid temperature.

24. Examination of transformation time after quenching is done in which temperature?

- At room temperature.

25. Isothermal transformations of eutectoid steel between 723oC and 550oC produces which microstructure?

- Pearlite.

26. Rapid quenching of eutectoid steel transforms the austenite into martensite at which temperature?

- Above 723°C.

27. Hot-quenching of eutectoid steels in austenitic condition results in formation of what?

- Bainite.

28. Bainite in iron-carbon alloys has a which structure?

- Non-lamellar.

29. Lower bainite is formed at which temperature range?

- 350-250°C.

30. Heterogeneous catalysis is also known as Surface Catalysis (true/false)

- TRUE

31. Homogeneous nucleation occurs much more often than Heterogeneous nucleation (true/false)

- FALSE

32. Heterogeneous nucleation is the process of nucleation that takes place away from the surface of the system (true/false)

- FALSE

33. Critical radius r* remains unchanged for heterogenous nucleation and homogeneous nucleation. (true/ false)

- TRUE

34. Heterogeneous nucleation applies to the phase transformation between any two phases of gas, liquid, or solid. (TRUE/FALSE)

- TRUE

35. Which Instrument provides vertical passage through which liquid material is introduced into a mold

- Sprue

36. How many axes of symmetry are present in cubic crystal system?

- 13

37. How many plane of symmetry are present in cubic crystal system?

- 9

38. What is the distance between the two layers of cubic closed packing crystal?

- $a/\sqrt{3}$

39. What is the packing efficiency of face centered cubic unit cell crystal system?

- 74.05%

40. Which compound shows both Frenkel and Schottky defects?

- AgBr

41. Dielectrics which show spontaneous polarization are called as

- Ferroelectric

42. Polarization in Ferroelectric materials is

- Reversible

43. All ferroelectric materials are pyroelectric and piezoelectric

- True

44. The temperature characteristic of every ferroelectric crystal is called

- Transition temperature

45. The dielectric constant if a ferroelectric material changes with

- Temperature

46. What happens in Ferroelectric material when $T<Tc$?

- Spontaneously polarized

47. The polarization left when the field is reduced to zero is called

- Residual polarization

48. Example of Non ferroelectric material

- The Phosphate

49. Rochelle salt is ferroelectric only in the temperature range 255 K to 296 K

- TRUE

50. The curie temperature for KH2PO4

- 123 K

51. Gibbs phase rule for general system:

- P+F=C+2

52. In a single-component condensed system, if degree of freedom is zero, maximum number of phases that can co-exist

- 2

53. The degree of freedom at triple point in unary diagram for water

- 0

54. Define Twin boundary.

- A twin boundary is a special type of grain boundary across which there is a specific mirror lattice symmetry;that is ,atoms on one side of the boundary are located in mirror image positions of the atoms on the other side.The region of material between these boundaries is appropriately termed a twin.

55. what is the cause of surface imperfection ?

- Surface imperfections arise from a change in the stacking of atomic planes on or across a boundary. The change may be one of the orientations or of the stacking sequences of atomic planes.

56. Not a Hume-Ruthery condition:

- Elements should form compounds with each other

57. The boundary line between (liquid) and (liquid+solid) regions must be part of

- Liquidus

58. The boundary line between (liquid+solid) and (solid) regions must be part of _

- Solidus

59. The boundary line between (alpha) and (alpha+beta) regions must be part of

- Solvus

60. Define the type of Grain boundaries as per their orientation.

- As per the orientation,Grain boundaries are of two type ; Low-angle grain boundaries : Low angle grain boundaries are those with a misorientation less than about 11 degrees. High-angle grain boundaries: High-angle grain boundaries are whose misorientation is greater than about 11 degrees.

61. Explain about Stacking fault in crystal.

- A stacking fault is a planar defect that can occur in crystalline materials. Crystalline materials form repeating patterns of layers of atoms.Stacking faults can arise during crystal growth or from plastic deformation.

62. How twin boundaries occurs ?

- Twin boundaries occur when two crystals of the same type intergrow so that only a slight misorientation exists between them.

63. Why Grain boundary have high energy ?

- The mismatch of the orientation of neighboring grains leads to a less efficient atomic packing within the grain boundary. Hence the atoms in the boundary have a less ordered structure and a slightly higher internal energy

64. Write three characteristics of Grain boundaries .

- i. Grain boundaries are the region of orientation mismatched.
ii.Grain boundaries are the region of high impurity concentration.
iii.Grain boundaries are region of low melting point temperature.

65. Is Axis of Symmetry a real line or an imaginary line?

- It's an imaginary line .

66. What do you mean by 2 fold axis of rotation?

- It means that in a rotation of 360° about a certain axis of the crystal, same appearance is repeated 2 times.

67. Does 5 fold and 7 fold rotation axis exist?

- 5 fold and 7 fold rotation axis does not exist.

68. Why rotation axes except 2,3,4,6-fold rotation axis does not exist?

- Although 5-fold, 7-fold and higher fold axes of rotation are possible in objects, they are not possible in crystals. The reason being that they cannot combine in such a way that they completely fill space. Some gaps in space are left.

69. How many axes of symmetry are present in a cubic crystal of NaCl?

- 13 axes of symmetry are present in a cubic crystal of NaCl.

70. How many 3-fold axes of symmetry are there in cubic crystal of NaCl?

- 4 three-fold axes of symmetry are there in a cubic crystal of NaCl.

71. How many 4-fold axes of symmetry are there in cubic crystal of NaCl?

- 3 four-fold axes of symmetry are there in a cubic crystal of NaCl.

72. How many 2-fold axes of symmetry are there in cubic crystal of NaCl?

- 6 two-fold axes of symmetry are there in a cubic crystal of NaCl.

73. What do you mean by 3 fold axis of rotation?

- It means that in a rotation of 360° about a certain axis of the crystal, same appearance is repeated 3 times.

74. What do you mean by 4 fold axis of rotation?

- It means that in a rotation of 360° about a certain axis of the crystal, same appearance is repeated 4 times.

75. What is the coordination no. Of HCP and CCP lattice?

- 12

76. Which type of crystal is brass ?

- Molecular crystal

77. Calculate the no. Of unit cells present in 1g of gold which have FCC lattice?

- 7.64×10^20

78. Solid X is a very hard electrical insulator in solid as well as in molten state.it melts at extremely high temperature. Determine type of Solid X?

- Covalent solid

79. An atom located at body center of a cubic unit cell is shared by how many other unit cells?

- 0

80. In CCP lattice what is the pattern of successive layer?

- ABC, ABC, ABC

81. What is the relation between height and radius of HCP lattice?

- $h=4r\sqrt{(2/3)}$

82. MgO has the structure of NaCl.What is the coordination no.of MgO?

- 6

83. How many no. Of tetrahedral void are in HCP?

- 12

84. What is the coordination no. Of AB having rocksalt structure?

- 6

85. Give an example of elastomers?

- Buna-s,Buna-N.

86. What does the part 6,6 mean in the name nylon-6,6?

- Adipic acid, Hexamethylenediamine.

87. What does the designation 6,6 mean in tha name nylons6,6?

- Since both adipic acid and hexamethylenediamine contain six carbon atoms each.

88. What is meant by 'copolymerisation??

- When two or more different monomers are allowed to polymerize together the product formed is called copolymerisation.

89. What are biodegradable polymers?

- All those polymers which disintegrate by themselves in biological systems during certain period of time by enzymatic hydrolysis are called biodegradable polymers.

90. Define the term, 'homopolymerisation ' ?

- The polymer formed by tha polymerization of a single/ same monomeric species is known as homopolymerezation.

91. Give an example of condensation polymer?

- Nylon 6,6.

92. which of the following is a natural polymer?

- Protein is a natural polymer.

93. Based on molecular forces what type of polymer is neoprene?

- Elastomers.

94. Which one of the following is a fibre?

- Nylon is a Fibre.

95. Define fundamental form of crystal system.

- It designated that type of any given form in which the parameters essentially correspond to the crystallographic axes.
A form having a symbol (111) is essentially a fundamental.

96. For orthorhombic system , axial ratio is $a \neq b \neq c$, what is the axial angle?

- The axial angle is alpha=beta=Gama=90°

97. Give an example of monoclinic system.

- Na_2SO_4

98. For hexagonal system axial angle is alpha=beta=90°,Gama=120°. What is their axial ratio?

- Axial ratio is $a=b \neq c$

99. Which steel would you choose for Cyclic stress application?

-Austenitic stainless steel

100. Which material property can be defined as its ability to resist a fluctuating or repetitive stress?
- fatigue strength

101. In how many types can a fatigue be classified ?Name them.
- "Fatigue is classified into five types namely

- 1.Cyclic Fatigue
- 2.Corrosion Fatigue
- 3.Fretting Fatigue
- 4.Thermal Fatigue
- 5.Acoustic Fatigue"

102. What is term referred to fatigue failure resulting from the strains caused by expansion and contraction in thermal cycling?

- Thermal Fatigue

103. The ability of materials to develop a characteristic behavior under repeated loading known as ___

- Fatigue

104. factors affecting impact strength?

- 1.temperature
- 2.thickness of material
- 3.notch radius

105. Types of failures

- 1.brittle fracture
- 2.slight cracking
- 3.ductile fracture
- 4. yielding

106. state the main differnce between charpy and izod test.

- The main difference between the Izod test and the Charpy test is the orientation of the specimen in the measuring equipment.

107. State the test to measure impact strength.

- charpy and izod test

108. What kind of material exhibits high impact strength?

- Materials with high yield strength and low modulus of elasticity

109. Write correct equation for phase rule

- F=C-P+2

110. Maximum degree of freedom for two component system is/are

- 3

111. The decomposition of caco3 in a closed vessel then find number of component and phases

- 3 and 2

112. A system containing liquid water and water vapour has the number of phases equal to

- 2

113. Phase rule is concerned with system

- Heterogeneous

114. At eutectic point in the two component system is

- Non-variant

115. A super saturated solution of Nacl is a

- Two-phase system

116. In ferric chloride water system the number of eutectic point are

- 5

117. In ferric chloride water system the number of congruent melting point are

- 4

118. At a triple point

- Both the temperature and pressure are fixed

119. Shock resistance of steel is increased by adding which material ?

- Nickel

120. Which material is used for producing laser ?

- Ruby

121. Which metal is used for galvanization of iron ?

- Zinc

122. When pure semiconductor is heated it's conductivity _________ ?

- Increases

123. What is material science?

- Material Science is an interdisciplinary field applying the synthesis, characterization and properties of material to various areas of science and engineering.

124. What are the uses of material science in engineering?

- Material science engineers work with diverse type of materials (e.g. metals, polymer, ceramics, liquid crystal, composites) for a broad range of application (e.g. energy, construction, electronics, biotechnology, nanotechnology etc.).

125. Crystal structure of material is generally examined by which technique ?

- X-ray technique

126. Repeatable entity of a crystal structure is known as ________ ?

- unitcell

127. Two types of non-stoichiometric defects are

- 1 metal excess defect
- 2 metal deficiency defect

128. A Frenkel defect changes the overall electrical neutrality of crystal. True or False?

- FALSE

129. Which kind of defect is dominant in alkali halides?

- Schottky

130. What's the result on enthalpy due to formation of point imperfections?

- it increases

131. The type of non-stoichiometric defect caused when solids have less number of metals relative to described stoichiometric proportion

- Metal deficiency defect

132. The defect in which a pair of 1 cation and 1 anion can be missing from an ionic crystal is called

- Schottky defect

133. How many kinds of space lattices are possible in a crystal?

- 14

134. In which arrangement the metal could have least density?

- Simple cubic

135. The total no of tetrahedral voids in FCC unit cell.

- 8

136. The crystal system in which all sides are equal and perpendicular.

- Cubic crystal system

137. The no of effective atoms in Body centered cubic unit cell.

- 2

138. The match box exhibits which geometry

- Orthorhombic geometry

139. What is the coordination number of body centered cubic unit cell

- 8

140. Copper posses which kind of close packing arrangement?

- Face centered cubic arrangement.

141. No of octahedral voids in body centered cubic unit cell.

- 2

142. The fraction of total volume occupied by the atoms present in simple cubic ic

- π/6

143. Mild steel can be converted to high carbon steel by which heat treatment process ?

- Carburizing

144. In Annealing, cooling is done in which medium ?

- Furnace

145. For steel, which property can be enhanced upon annealing ?

- Ductility

146. Which is the hardest constituent of steel ?

- Martensite

147. Upon annealing, eutectoid steel converts to ___________

- Perlite

148. Which process we will use on hardened steel to reduce brittleness ?

- Tempering

149. What is to be done to sample as the first step in constructing a TTT diagram ?

- Austenising

150. What is the percentage of carbon in high carbon steels ?

- 0.5% to 0.7%

151. What is used to predict hardening reactions in steel ?

- TTT Diagram (Isothermal Transformation Diagram)

152. Which process is used for producing high strength ropes and piano wires ?

- Patenting

153. What type of defect can arise when a solid is heated ?

- Vacancy defects can arise when a solid is heated.

154. Why does LiCl acquire pink colour when heated in Li vapours?

- This is due to metal excess defect due to anionic vacancies in which the anionic sites are occupied by unpaired electrons (F-centres).

155. Which ionic compound shows both Frenkel and Schottky defects?

- Silver bromide (AgBr).

156. Which type of ionic substances show Schottky defect in solids?

- Highly ionic compounds with high coordination number and small difference in size of cations and anions show schottky defect.

157. What is crystal planes?

- Any set of parallel Planes that may be supposed to pass through the centre of atoms in crystal

158. How to designate the orientation and direction of these parallel Planes?

- By Miller indices

159. What is Miller indices?

- It is a system of notation for specifying direction and planes

160. Which symbol is used in Miller indices?

- hkl

161. For what square bracket is used in Miller indices?

- To designate the direction

162. For what small bracket is used in Miller indices?

- To designate the plane

163. Can we separate these indices "hkl" by comma ?

- No

164. When will we use comma in Miller indices ?

- Whenever the value of Miller indices come in double digits i.e (10,15,11)

165. Pearlite is a combination of

- Ferrite (87.5 wt%) and cementite (12.5 wt%)

166. Which material in the final structure of steel increase the strength of steel?

- Martensite

167. Case hardening is method of producing hard skin on the structure of

- Low carbon steel parts

168. Material is heated in which temperature during the normalizing process?

- 750 - 980°c (1320 - 1796°F)

169. Which surface hardening process needs no quenching?

- Nitriding

170. What is defined as the ability of the structure to transform into martensite?

- Hardenability

171. Which process is used on hardened steel to reduce brittleness?

- Tempering

172. In annealing process,the cooling rate of carbon steel is

- 100- 150°c/HR

173. In martempering , steel is quenched at which temperature

- 150 - 300°c

174. Which process is used to austenite transforms isothermally to lower bainite?

- Austempering

175. When writing the index for a set of symmetrically related planes, which type of brackets should be used?

- {Curly} brackets should be used while writing the indexes for a set of symmetrically related planes.

176. Miller indices for a Octahedral plane in cubic crystal?

- The Miller indices for a Octahedral plane in cubic crystal are denoted by (111).

177. A family of directions is represented by?

- A set of directions related by symmetry operations of the lattice or the crystal is called family of directions. They are represented by <uvw>.

178. Repeatable entity of a crystal structure is known as?

- The repeatable entity of a crystal structure is known as unit cell.

179. Can Miller indices be infinite?

- The Miller indices are proportional to the inverse of the intercepts of the plane, in the basis of the lattice vectors. If one of the indices is zero, it means that the planes do not intersect that axis(the intercept is at infinity).

180. Why do we use Miller indices?

- Miller indices are used to specify directions and planes. These directions and planes could be in lattices Or in crystal. The number of indices will match with the dimension of the lattice or the crystal.

181. Can Miller indices for the perpendicular planes be same?

- Miller indices for the perpendicular planes are always same.

182. What is the packing fraction for BCC crystal lattice?

- The packing fraction for BCC crystal lattice is 0.68%.

183. What is Miller bravais indices?

- The bravais -Miller indices are used in the case of hexagonal lattices. In that case one uses four axes a1, a2, a3, c and four Miller indices (hkil).

184. How do we find the Miller indices from intercepts?

- a) Identify the intercepts on the x-,y-and z-axes.
- b) specify the intercepts in fractional coordinates.
- c) Take the reciporcals of the fractional intercept.

185. Classical free electron theory was developed by whom?

- Drude and Lorentz

186. The average distance travelled by an electron between two successive collision is what?

- Mean free path

187. Does random motion of electrons produce current?

- No

188. How is current density related to electric field strength

- Current density= conductivity× electric field strength

189. How can crystal faces be defined on the crystallographic axes?

- By intercepts

190. How many parameters can be there for non-hexagonal crystals?

- 3

191. Parameters indicate actual cutting values of the crystallographic axes. True/False.

- FALSE

192. What is the largest face that intersects all the 3 crystallographic axes called?

- Unit face

193. What are the parameters of unit face?

- 1a, 1b, 1c

194. How can the parameters of each crystal face be uniquely identified ?

- Using Miller Indices

195. What is a set of crystal faces that are related to each other by symmetry called?

- Crystal form

196. If the face is moved parallel to itself, the parameters remained unchanged ,why?

- Because parameters are relative values.

197.What is the notation that is used to designate a crystal form, Miller Bravais notation enclosing the curly braces called?

- Form Symbol

198.How many types of Rhombic-Dipyramid Crystals are there?

- Two types(Both have different form symbols)

199.When kind of plane leads to symmetry in crystals?

- Imaginary plane

200. The equal portions divided by the plane are _______________

- Mirror images

Printed by Libri Plureos GmbH in Hamburg,
Germany